16

NATURAL RESOURCES

Jack and Meg Gillett
With contributions by Richard and Louise Spilsbury

WAYLAND

Contents

About this book

This book looks at the natural resources that are found and used around the world. These include essentials, such as water and food, but also natural resources such as metals that make bicycles, mobile phones and other things that we enjoy having, but can live without.

The location of a country determines what natural resources it has and the distribution of these resources affect a country's development. For example, some countries with plenty of mineral resources have developed industries that turn those minerals into products.

There is a limited amount of most of the Earth's natural resources and one day they will run out. Digging up or obtaining these resources can damage or destroy habitats. Also, processing raw materials into products uses large amounts of energy, which causes pollution and contributes to climate change. In the future, it will become increasingly important to find alternative ways of sourcing natural resources, such as recycling.

Each double page in this book introduces the location and distribution of natural resources in a different region of the world. A map locates relevant sites and graphs and statistics provide important data. At the end of the book is a section you can use for further study and comparisons.

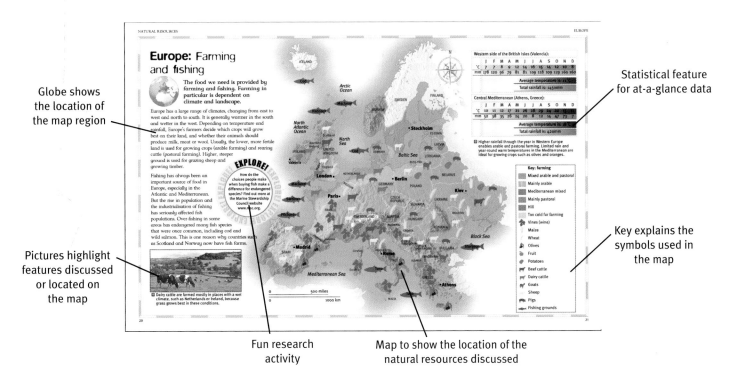

Globe shows the location of the map region

Pictures highlight features discussed or located on the map

Fun research activity

Map to show the location of the natural resources discussed

Statistical feature for at-a-glance data

Key explains the symbols used in the map

The world: Water supply

Water is an essential natural resource. People can survive for three weeks without food, but may die after three days without water. We need water to live, to cook, keep clean, grow crops and raise livestock. People also use water for non-essential purposes. Industrialised countries use vast amounts of water in factories and power stations, and in things like washing machines and swimming pools.

There is a limited, or finite, amount of water on Earth and people in different locations have a different share of it. Water availability is mainly affected by climate. Places with hot, dry climates, such as deserts, have little rainfall. Places with rainy seasons have more water and can store surplus water in reservoirs. In some places water is polluted, so cannot be safely used by people without expensive treatment. With a rising global population, and increasing non-essential water use, supplying enough water for everyone is a major challenge in the 21st century.

NORTH AMERICA

Mojave Desert

Sonoran Desert

SOUTH AMERICA

Atacama Desert

Monte Desert

6 billion
World population

0.5 billion
Chronically short of water

Year 2000

8.9 billion
World population

4 billion
Chronically short of water

Year 2050 (projected)

⬆ By 2050, experts predict that nearly half the world's population will have a chronic water shortage. This means they will not have enough to remain healthy.

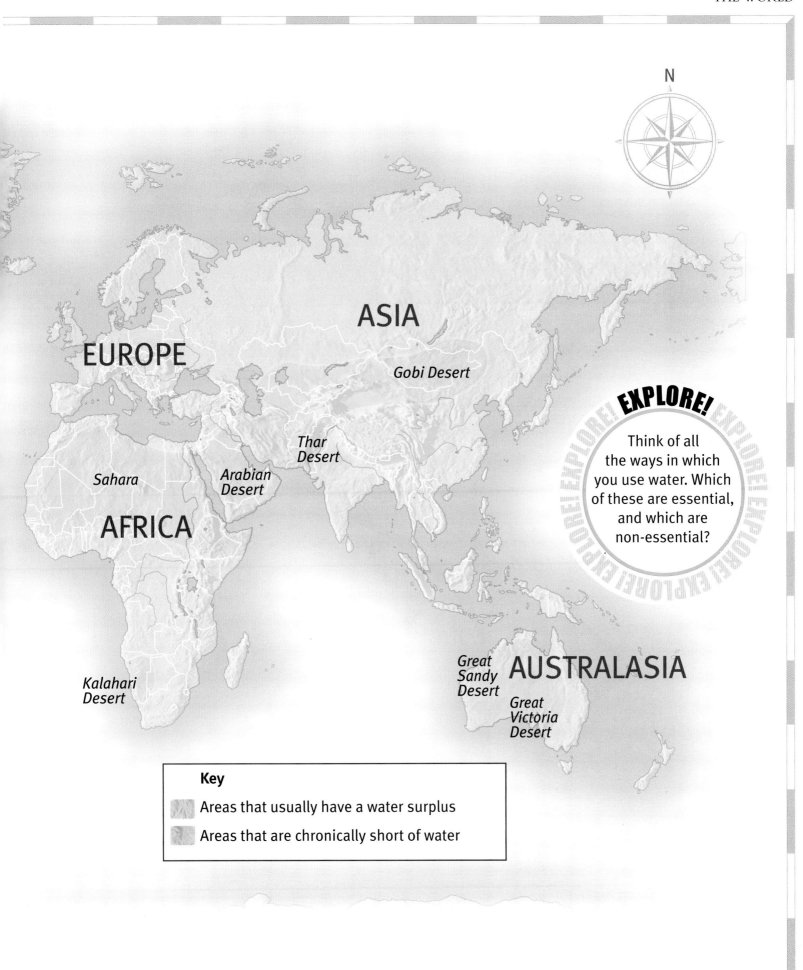

N

ASIA

EUROPE

Gobi Desert

EXPLORE!

Think of all
the ways in which
you use water. Which
of these are essential,
and which are
non-essential?

Thar
Desert

Sahara

Arabian
Desert

AFRICA

Great
Sandy
Desert

AUSTRALASIA

Kalahari
Desert

Great
Victoria
Desert

Key

Areas that usually have a water surplus

Areas that are chronically short of water

The world: Fossil fuels

Coal, gas and oil are natural resources that we call fossil fuels. They formed from the remains of plants and animals that lived millions of years ago. We mostly use these resources to generate useful energy.

Coal is mostly burned in power stations to generate electricity. Gas is also used in power stations, as well as being piped into homes to use for heating and cooking. Petrol and diesel made from oil are essential to make the engines in cars, aeroplanes and ships work. We use enormous amounts of energy and this is rising each year because of the growing world population and increased use of vehicles and electricity in modern life.

Some countries have more fossil fuel reserves than others, but all fossil fuels will run out one day. Another problem is that burning fossil fuels causes pollution. This is why people are looking for alternative, sustainable energy resources, such as water, wind and solar (sun) power.

⬆ This bar graph shows how many years we can still use each fossil fuel (as of 2009).

⬆ Oil refineries changes crude oil from underground into fuels and many other by-products such as plastics.

N

Iceland

Norway
Sweden
Finland

Russian Federation

ASIA

UK

EUROPE
Ukraine
Kazakhstan
Mongolia
Japan

France

Spain

Turkey

China

Morocco
Algeria
Libya
Egypt
Iraq
Iran
Saudi
Arabia
Pakistan

India

Mali
Niger
Chad
Sudan

Thailand

Nigeria

AFRICA
Ethiopia
Malaysia

Dem.
Repub.
of Congo

Indonesia
Papua
New
Guinea

Angola
Zambia

Madagascar

Namibia
Australia
AUSTRALASIA

South
Africa

New
Zealand

Key

Oil field

Coalfield

Gas field

EXPLORE!

Find out which of the three fossil fuels pollutes the air the most. Which pollutes the air the least?

Antarctica

Europe: Metallic minerals

Metallic minerals are natural substances from the Earth from which we get metals such as copper and iron. These metals are used to produce many of the products we use in everyday life including aeroplanes, bridges and computers.

Different amounts and types of metals are found in rocks called ores in different locations worldwide. The Industrial Revolution began in Europe because of the metallic minerals there. The region also had fossil fuels to power machines and factories that turned the raw materials into products, such as ships and railways.

There is a limited supply of metallic minerals and they are being used up as people buy more and develop new metal products. For example, silver, used for electronics and jewellery, could run out by 2020. We can recycle some metals by melting and reusing them. It takes five tonnes of bauxite ore to make one tonne of new aluminium, but none to make recycled aluminium.

⬆ This steelworks in Sheffield, UK, uses iron ore found nearby to make steel and local coal to power its machines.

EXPLORE!

Find out which metallic minerals are used to produce the following products: mobile phone, car, computer and fridge.

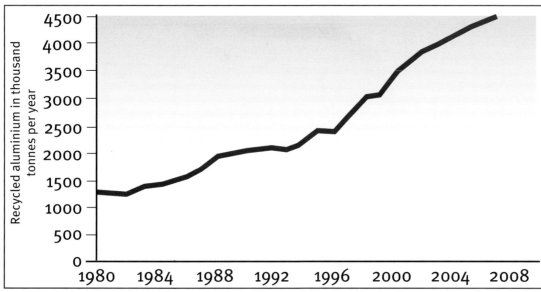

⬆ This graph shows how much aluminium has been recycled in Europe since 1980. The amount is increasing, currently reaching to around 90 per cent of drinks cans. Today, Europe is a global leader in recycling metals along with North America and Japan.

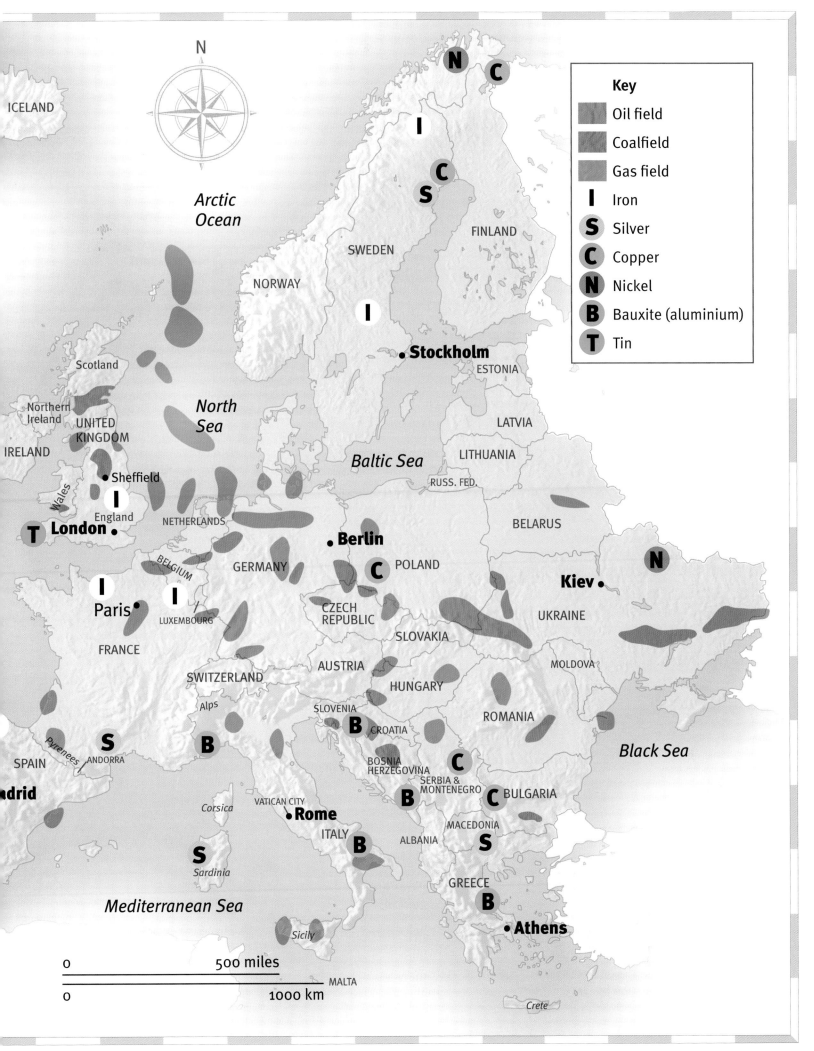

ICELAND

Arctic
Ocean

N

Key
- Oil field
- Coalfield
- Gas field
- **I** Iron
- **S** Silver
- **C** Copper
- **N** Nickel
- **B** Bauxite (aluminium)
- **T** Tin

N   C

I

C
S

FINLAND

SWEDEN

NORWAY

I

• **Stockholm**

ESTONIA

Scotland

North
Sea

LATVIA

Northern
Ireland

UNITED
KINGDOM

Baltic Sea

LITHUANIA

IRELAND

RUSS. FED.

Wales

• Sheffield

I

England

BELARUS

T **London**   •

NETHERLANDS

• **Berlin**

BELGIUM

GERMANY

C

POLAND

Kiev •

I

I

Paris •

LUXEMBOURG

CZECH
REPUBLIC

UKRAINE

FRANCE

SLOVAKIA

MOLDOVA

SWITZERLAND

AUSTRIA

HUNGARY

Alps

SLOVENIA

B

CROATIA

ROMANIA

Black Sea

SPAIN

Pyrenees

ANDORRA

S

B

BOSNIA
HERZEGOVINA

C

SERBIA &
MONTENEGRO

Madrid

B

C   BULGARIA

Corsica

VATICAN CITY

• **Rome**

MACEDONIA

ITALY

B

ALBANIA

S

S

Sardinia

GREECE

Mediterranean Sea

B

Sicily

• **Athens**

0		500 miles

MALTA

0		1000 km

Crete

9

The British Isles:
Building materials

Large amounts of natural resources are used to construct houses and other buildings. These include stone and clay to make bricks, and sand to make concrete and glass.

People used to build their houses using local natural resources because building materials are heavy and so they are difficult and expensive to move a long way. In the British Isles, wood was widely used because most of the area was covered by forest, but when forests were depleted people used stone. They used different types of stone depending on location. In Cornwall many houses are made from granite and in Yorkshire many were built of millstone grit. Nowadays, concrete and bricks are the most common building materials in the British Isles.

Deep quarries have been dug to obtain stone using heavy machinery and explosives. These leave giant holes in the landscape. There is more stone for future use, but to extract it will destroy even more land.

Natural resources	Building uses
Chalk	Cements
Clay	Bricks, pipes, roof tiles
Flint, granite, limestone, sandstone, slate	Walls of buildings and between fields
Gravel	Roads, paths and pebble-dash on walls
Lead	Church roofs
Limestone	Cement
Sand	Cement, glass, mortar
Slate	Roofs
Steel	Girders to support large buildings
Tarmac	Paths, roads
Wood	Doors, roof supports, window frames

⬆ This table shows the most common building materials, and what they are used for.

EXPLORE! Find out what your school building is made of, and where its building materials came from.

⬆ This cottage in Conwy, north Wales, was built with slate. Slate can be 'sliced' to make roof tiles, too.

⬆ Millstone grit describes all types of sandstone. It is used for houses, such as this one in Halifax, and in the past as grindstones in mills.

⬆ Flint is a small, pebble-like stone. It is used for many buildings in south-east England, like this church in Ramsgate.

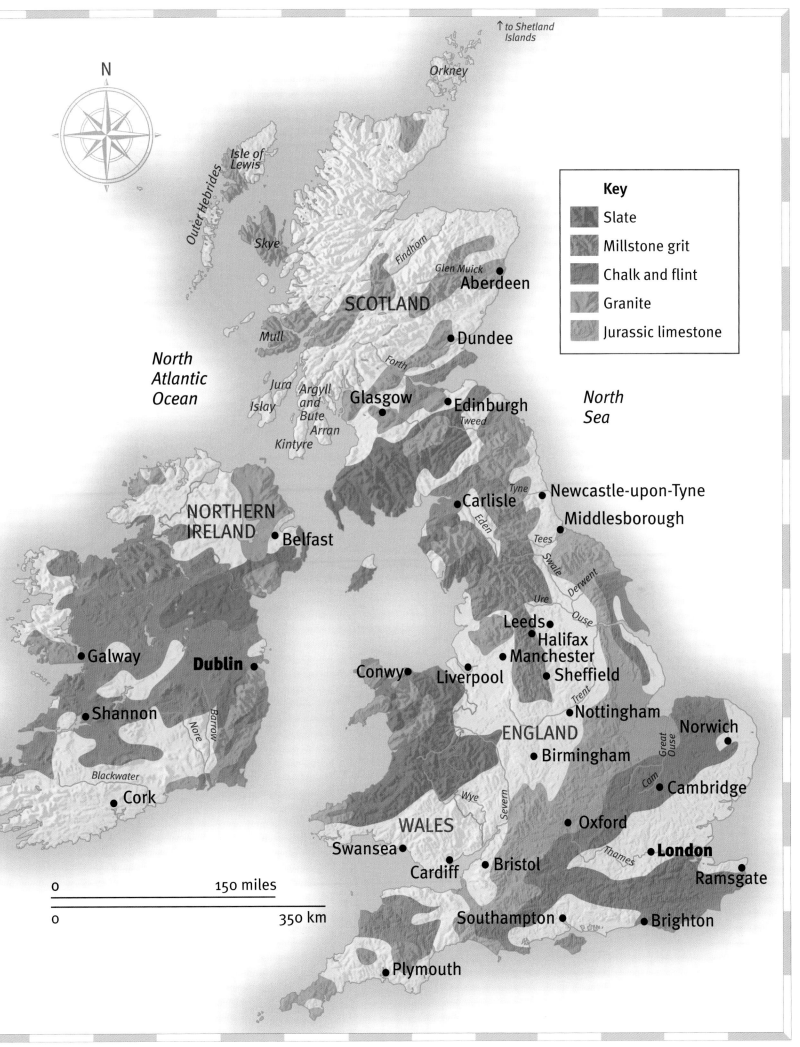

N

↑ to Shetland Islands

Orkney

Isle of Lewis

Outer Hebrides

Skye

Key
Slate
Millstone grit
Chalk and flint
Granite
Jurassic limestone

Findhorn

Glen Muick

Aberdeen

SCOTLAND

Mull

Dundee

North Atlantic Ocean

Forth

Jura

Islay

Argyll and Bute

Arran

Kintyre

Glasgow

Edinburgh

Tweed

North Sea

Carlisle

Newcastle-upon-Tyne

Middlesborough

NORTHERN IRELAND

Belfast

Eden

Tyne

Tees

Swale

Derwent

Ure

Ouse

Galway

Dublin

Leeds

Halifax

Manchester

Conwy

Liverpool

Sheffield

Shannon

Nore

Barrow

Trent

Nottingham

ENGLAND

Norwich

Great Ouse

Birmingham

Blackwater

Cam

Cambridge

Cork

Wye

Severn

WALES

Oxford

Swansea

Cardiff

Bristol

Thames

London

Ramsgate

Southampton

Brighton

Plymouth

0   150 miles

0   350 km

Africa: Precious metals and stones

Precious metals and stones are rare and valuable minerals. Apart from jewellery, these natural resources are used in other ways, too. For example, hard diamonds are used to make cutting and drilling tools and gold is used in electronics.

Africa is rich in precious stones and metals. South Africa has large amounts of gold and diamonds. Like metallic minerals, most of these precious minerals have to be mined and dug out from under the ground, causing environmental damage.

Some parts of Africa are able to grow food and other crops such as cotton, but generally farming is difficult because of the hot and dry climate. In fact, deserts (see map on pages 4–5) are spreading, mainly due to climate change, causing hardship in drier regions. This is why a lot of African countries are so reliant on the trade and export of precious metals and stones.

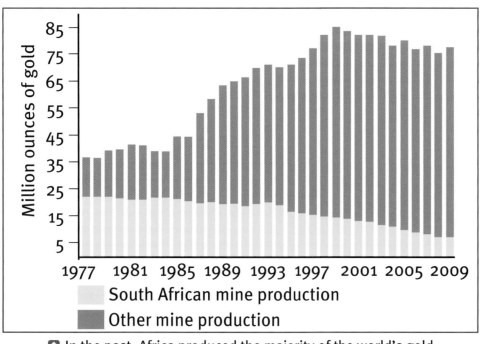

South African mine production

Other mine production

⬆ In the past, Africa produced the majority of the world's gold, but the amount it produces today is falling because supplies are running out.

EXPLORE!

Which African countries produce tantalum? What is it used for and why is demand growing?

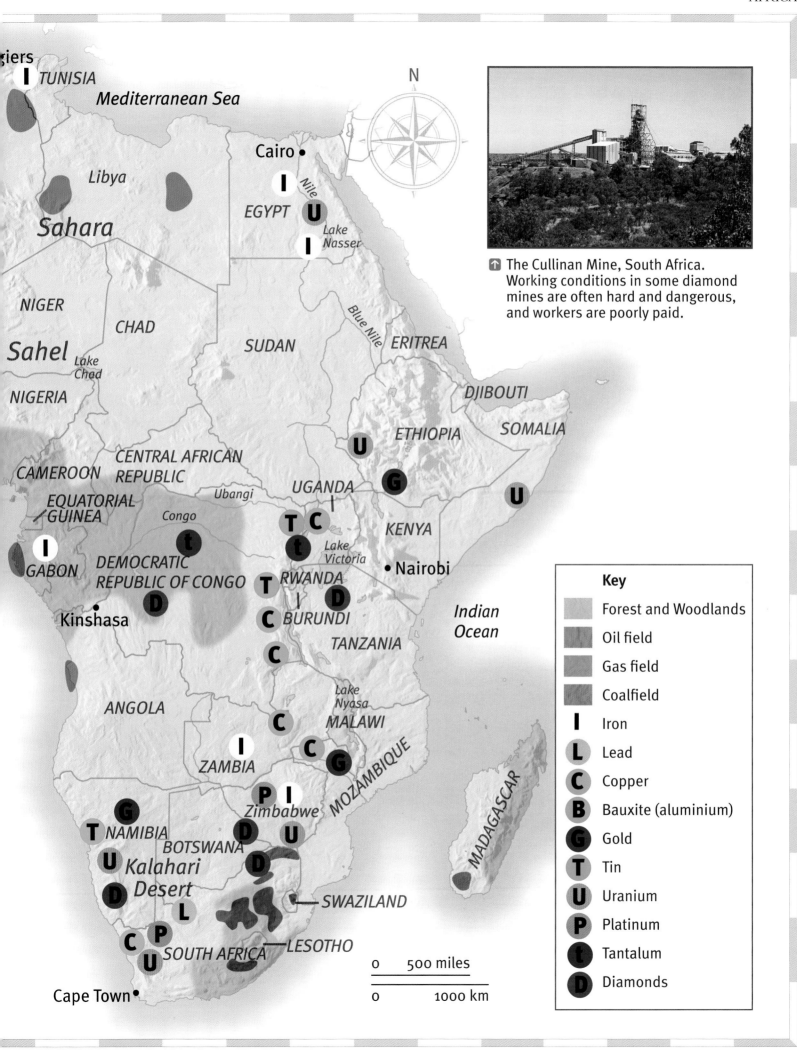

giers

I TUNISIA

Mediterranean Sea

Cairo •

I

U

Nile

EGYPT

I

Lake Nasser

Libya

Sahara

NIGER

CHAD

Sahel

Lake Chad

SUDAN

Blue Nile

ERITREA

DJIBOUTI

NIGERIA

CENTRAL AFRICAN REPUBLIC

Ubangi

U

ETHIOPIA

SOMALIA

CAMEROON

EQUATORIAL GUINEA

Congo

t

UGANDA

G

U

I

GABON

DEMOCRATIC REPUBLIC OF CONGO

T **C**

t

KENYA

Kinshasa •

D

T RWANDA

D

Lake Victoria

• Nairobi

T **C**

BURUNDI

Indian Ocean

C

TANZANIA

ANGOLA

C

Lake Nyasa

MALAWI

Key

Forest and Woodlands

I

ZAMBIA

C

G

MOZAMBIQUE

Oil field

Gas field

Coalfield

G

P **I**

Zimbabwe

MADAGASCAR

I Iron

T NAMIBIA

D **U**

L Lead

U

BOTSWANA

D

C Copper

D Kalahari Desert

SWAZILAND

B Bauxite (aluminium)

L

G Gold

C **P**

SOUTH AFRICA

LESOTHO

T Tin

U

U Uranium

Cape Town •

0   500 miles

P Platinum

0   1000 km

t Tantalum

D Diamonds

⬆ The Cullinan Mine, South Africa. Working conditions in some diamond mines are often hard and dangerous, and workers are poorly paid.

N

North America: Industrial raw materials

Industrial raw materials are resources such as metals and fuels that are used to make products in factories. These are then sold within a country or exported. For example, lead is used to make batteries and oil can be used to make plastic.

North America contains many industrial raw materials. It also has the fossil fuels needed to extract those resources and to power the factories that turn them into products. Having plentiful natural resources has helped to make the USA the richest nation in the world, and Canada one of the world's richer, More Economically Developed Countries (MEDCs).

Among North America's big industries are car manufacturers Ford, Chrysler and General Motors, aircraft builder Boeing, and Microsoft, which is a world leader in computer technology. Canada has a smaller population than the USA, and its wealth comes more from extracting and exporting raw materials than using them.

← Many of Canada's copper, iron ore and uranium mines are in its frozen, northern, wilderness area. This is an iron ore mine in Labrador.

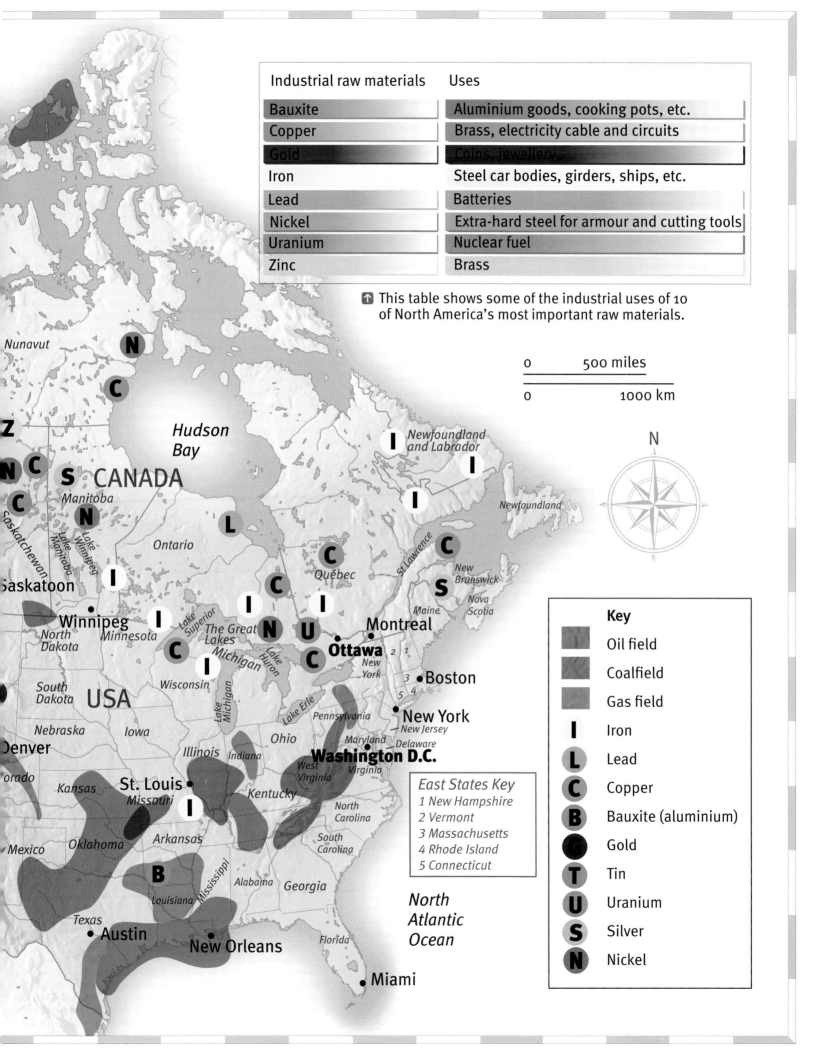

Industrial raw materials	Uses
Bauxite	Aluminium goods, cooking pots, etc.
Copper	Brass, electricity cable and circuits
Gold	Coins, jewellery
Iron	Steel car bodies, girders, ships, etc.
Lead	Batteries
Nickel	Extra-hard steel for armour and cutting tools
Uranium	Nuclear fuel
Zinc	Brass

⬆ This table shows some of the industrial uses of 10 of North America's most important raw materials.

0   500 miles

0   1000 km

N

Nunavut

Hudson Bay

CANADA

Manitoba

Saskatchewan

Saskatoon

Winnipeg

North Dakota

Minnesota

South Dakota

USA

Nebraska

Iowa

Denver

Colorado

Kansas

St. Louis

Missouri

Mexico

Oklahoma

Arkansas

Texas

Austin

Louisiana

Mississippi

New Orleans

Alabama

Georgia

Florida

Miami

Lake Winnipeg

Lake Manitoba

Ontario

Québec

Lake Superior

The Great Lakes

Lake Michigan

Lake Huron

Lake Erie

Wisconsin

Illinois

Indiana

Ohio

Michigan

Montreal

Ottawa

New York

Pennsylvania

New Jersey

Maryland

Delaware

Washington D.C.

West Virginia

Virginia

Kentucky

North Carolina

South Carolina

Tennessee

Newfoundland and Labrador

Newfoundland

St Lawrence

New Brunswick

Nova Scotia

Maine

Boston

New York

Newfoundland

North Atlantic Ocean

East States Key
1 New Hampshire
2 Vermont
3 Massachusetts
4 Rhode Island
5 Connecticut

Key	
	Oil field
	Coalfield
	Gas field
I	Iron
L	Lead
C	Copper
B	Bauxite (aluminium)
G	Gold
T	Tin
U	Uranium
S	Silver
N	Nickel

The Poles: Gas and oil

As amounts of available fossil fuels diminish, more remote parts of the world including the Poles are becoming more important as providers of these resources. Antarctica is an icy continent so cold and windy that few people live there except research scientists.

Antarctic waters are rich in fish and other animals that many penguins and whales feed on. Oil and gas are mostly found deep underwater too, where exploration and drilling are risky. They need to be carefully and sustainably carried out to avoid pollution and coastal damage affecting ocean wildlife.

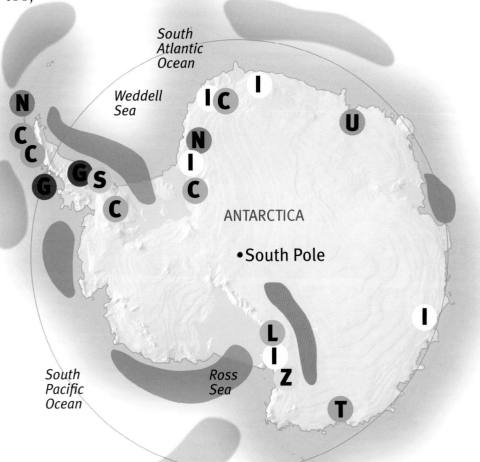

⬆ The ocean surrounding Antarctica is very rich in marine life. Killing whales there for food is illegal, but some countries still do it even though it endangers the whale population.

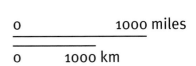

0   1000 miles

0   1000 km

Key

▢ Main whale feeding areas

▢ Oil and gas fields

▢ Coalfield

See p. 15 for minerals and metals key

See p. 15 for minerals and metals key

South Pole Location:

	J	F	M	A	M	J	J	A	S	O	N	D
°C	-32	-44	-58	-65	-66	-65	-68	-69	-66	-57	-32	-55
mm	0.1	0	0.7	0.5	0.4	0.5	0.6	0.7	0.3	0.2	0.1	0

Average temperature is: -60 ˚C

Total rainfall is: 4mm

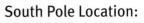

⬅ Antarctica has the world's coldest temperatures but strong winds make it feel even colder! Rain falls as snow around the coast, but central places such as the South Pole are as dry as deserts.

The Arctic is a region of frozen ocean surrounded by the coldest parts of Asia, Europe and North America.

Arctic oil and gas reserves have been drilled mostly on these continents. Any oil spills from pipes and tankers take longer to naturally clear away in cold waters. Therefore, Arctic pollution can stick around for a long time.

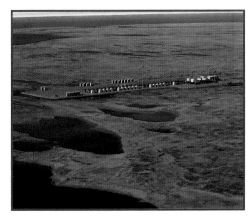

⬆ Coastal Alaska has some of the USA's richest oil fields. With global warming, oil companies will be able to drill further out into the Arctic Ocean because less of its surface is freezing over each year.

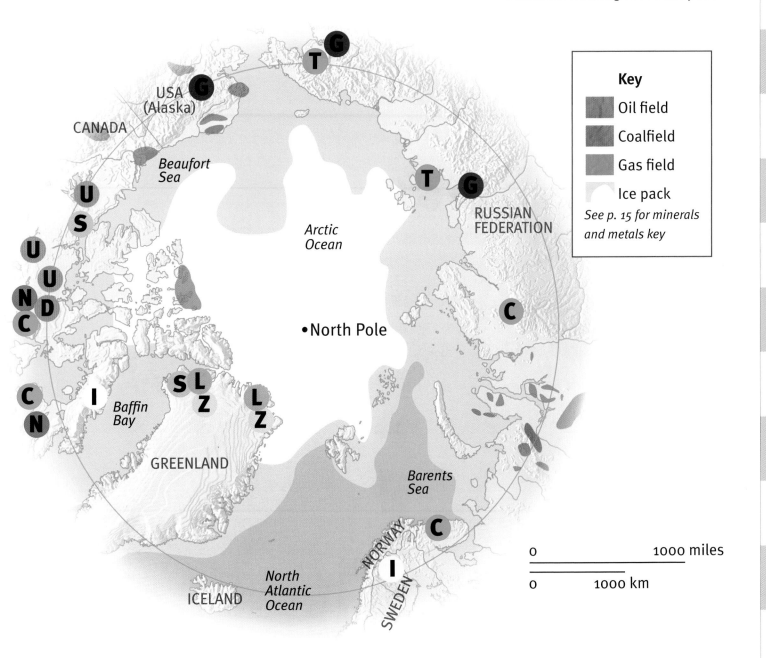

Key

Oil field

Coalfield

Gas field

Ice pack

See p. 15 for minerals and metals key

The world: Forests and forest products

We need wood for construction, paper, cardboard, musical instruments and many other products. People harvest wood from naturally growing forests and from plantations.

Hardwoods, used to make plywood and furniture, come from slow-growing trees. These include mahogany and teak, that grow in humid tropical rainforests, and oak and beech from cooler deciduous woodland. Fast-growing coniferous trees such as spruce and pine grow best in cold climates. Large areas of forest worldwide are being chopped down to meet the rising demand for timber. This is called deforestation.

Wood is not a finite resource, but trees take years, decades or, in the case of some hardwoods, centuries to grow. People are not using this resource sustainably where land is deforested quicker than it is replanted. Deforestation also affects the atmosphere. Trees use up carbon dioxide to make the oxygen most living things need to breathe. With fewer trees, there is less oxygen and more carbon dioxide that traps heat, causing global warming.

⬆ These mahogany rainforest trees took over a hundred years to grow. Their hardwood can be used to make expensive furniture.

Greenland

Alaska (USA)

Canada

NORTH AMERICA

USA

Mexico

Venezuela

Colombia

Ecuador

Peru

SOUTH AMERICA

Brazil

Bolivia

Paraguay

Uruguay

Chile

Argentina

EXPLORE!

Every year, 0.2 per cent of the world's forests are chopped down and not replaced. At this rate of deforestation, how many years will its forests last?

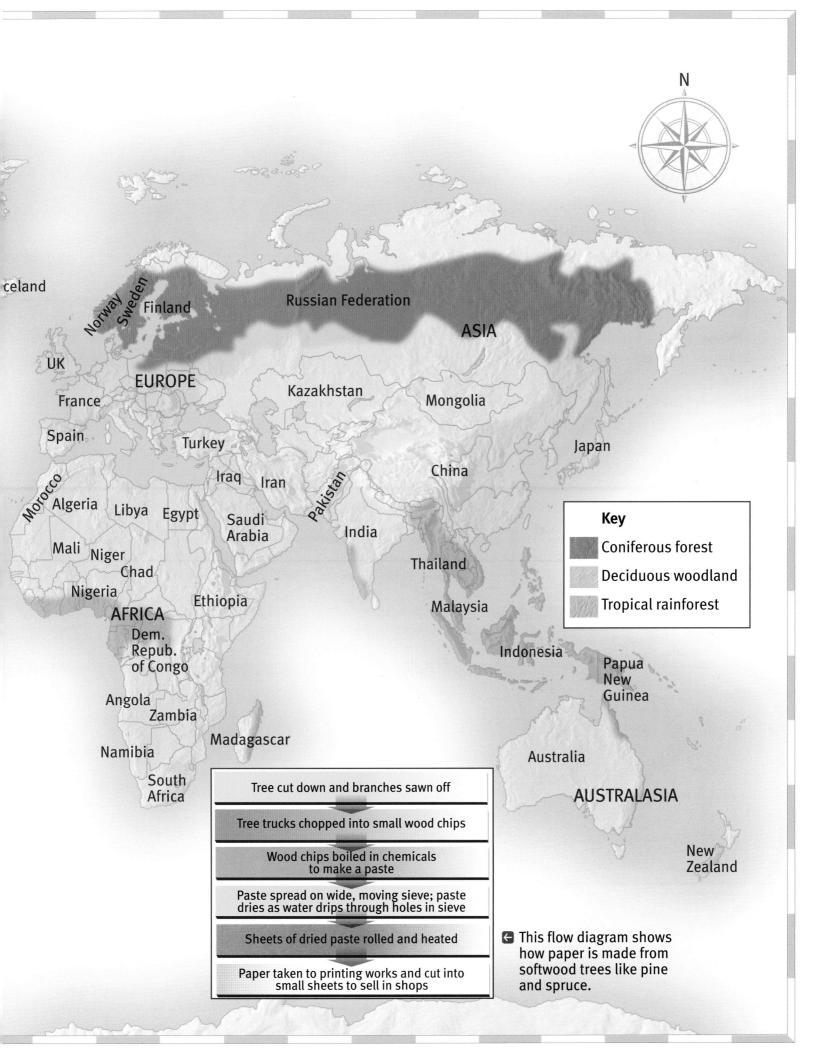

N

Key
- Coniferous forest
- Deciduous woodland
- Tropical rainforest

Iceland

Norway
Sweden
Finland
Russian Federation
ASIA

UK
EUROPE
Kazakhstan
Mongolia

France
Japan

Spain
Turkey
China

Morocco
Iraq Iran
Pakistan

Algeria Libya Egypt
Saudi Arabia
India

Mali Niger
Thailand

Chad
Nigeria
Ethiopia
Malaysia

AFRICA
Dem. Repub. of Congo
Indonesia
Papua New Guinea

Angola
Zambia

Namibia
Madagascar
Australia
AUSTRALASIA

South Africa
New Zealand

Tree cut down and branches sawn off

Tree trucks chopped into small wood chips

Wood chips boiled in chemicals to make a paste

Paste spread on wide, moving sieve; paste dries as water drips through holes in sieve

Sheets of dried paste rolled and heated

Paper taken to printing works and cut into small sheets to sell in shops

This flow diagram shows how paper is made from softwood trees like pine and spruce.

Europe: Farming and fishing

The food we need is provided by farming and fishing. Farming in particular is dependent on climate and landscape.

Europe has a large range of climates, changing from east to west and north to south. It is generally warmer in the south and wetter in the west. Depending on temperature and rainfall, Europe's farmers decide which crops will grow best on their land, and whether their animals should produce milk, meat or wool. Usually, the lower, more fertile land is used for growing crops (arable farming) and rearing cattle (pastoral farming). Higher, steeper ground is used for grazing sheep and growing timber.

Fishing has always been an important source of food in Europe, especially in the Atlantic and Mediterranean. But the rise in population and the industrialisation of fishing has seriously affected fish populations. Over-fishing in some areas has endangered many fish species that were once common, including cod and wild salmon. This is one reason why countries such as Scotland and Norway now have fish farms.

EXPLORE!

How do the choices people make when buying fish make a difference for endangered species? Find out more at the Marine Stewardship Council website www.msc.org.

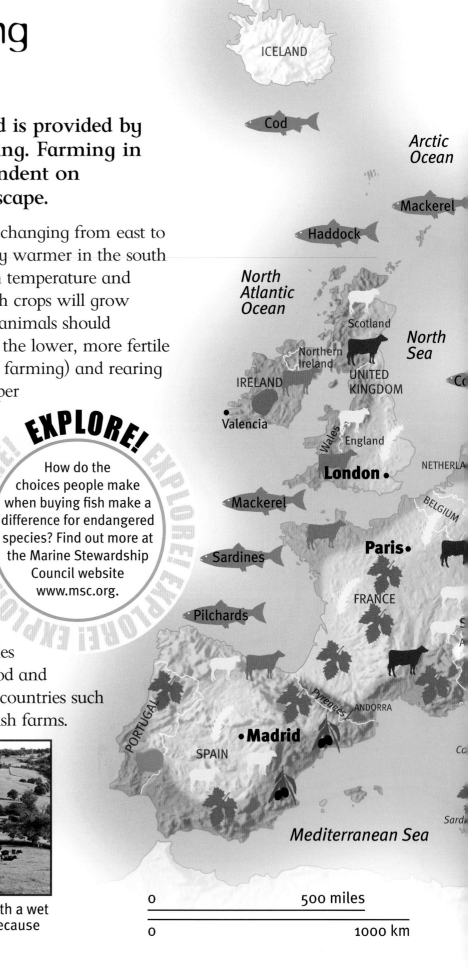

⬆ Dairy cattle are farmed mostly in places with a wet climate, such as Netherlands or Ireland, because grass grows best in these conditions.

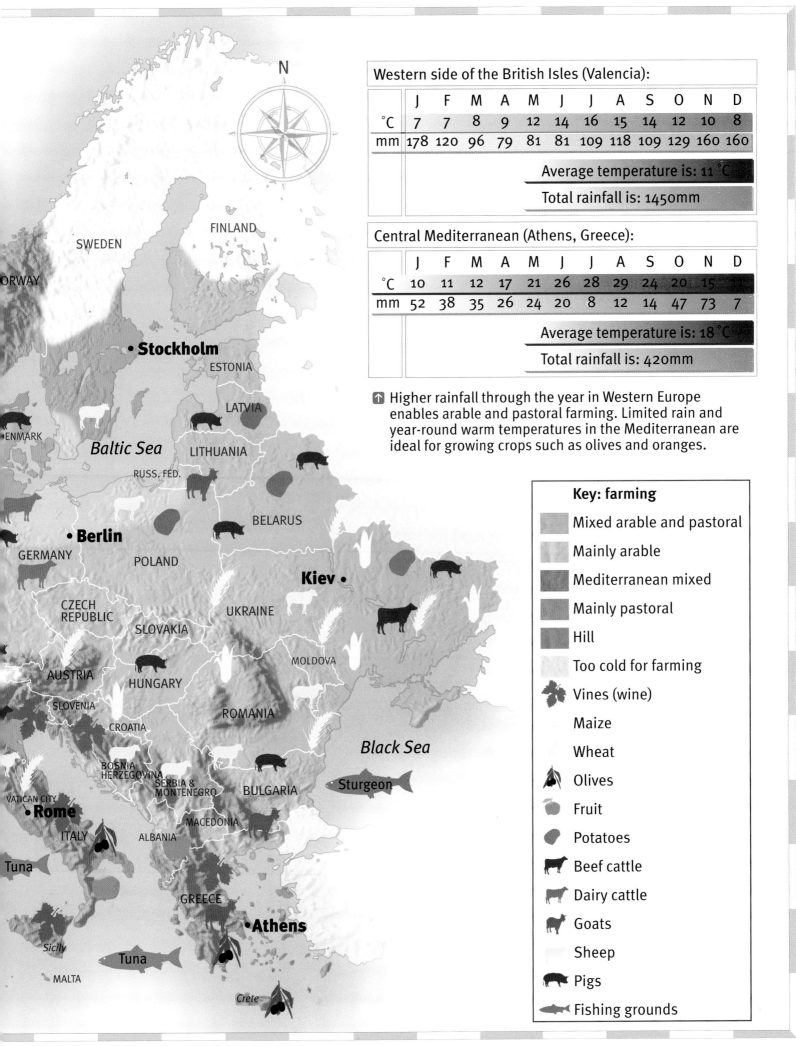

Western side of the British Isles (Valencia):

	J	F	M	A	M	J	J	A	S	O	N	D
°C	7	7	8	9	12	14	16	15	14	12	10	8
mm	178	120	96	79	81	81	109	118	109	129	160	160

Average temperature is: 11 °C

Total rainfall is: 1450mm

Central Mediterranean (Athens, Greece):

	J	F	M	A	M	J	J	A	S	O	N	D
°C	10	11	12	17	21	26	28	29	24	20	15	11
mm	52	38	35	26	24	20	8	12	14	47	73	7

Average temperature is: 18 °C

Total rainfall is: 420mm

⬆ Higher rainfall through the year in Western Europe enables arable and pastoral farming. Limited rain and year-round warm temperatures in the Mediterranean are ideal for growing crops such as olives and oranges.

Key: farming

- Mixed arable and pastoral
- Mainly arable
- Mediterranean mixed
- Mainly pastoral
- Hill
- Too cold for farming
- Vines (wine)
- Maize
- Wheat
- Olives
- Fruit
- Potatoes
- Beef cattle
- Dairy cattle
- Goats
- Sheep
- Pigs
- Fishing grounds

South-East Asia:
Monoculture

Monoculture farming is growing a single crop, such as palm oil, over a wide area. In South-East Asia the main monoculture crops in many countries are rice and rubber.

Rice is a staple food in South-East Asia — it is the main part of the diet for most people. South-East Asia has warm temperatures and plentiful rain to keep rice roots wet, which are ideal conditions for growing large amounts of rice. Rice is farmed in flat valleys but also on small terraces cut into mountainsides, with mud walls to trap rainwater. Around 75 per cent of global rice production is in South-East Asia, and China is the major world producer.

Rubber trees are widely grown on large plantations in South-East Asia. A milky liquid called latex containing rubber is produced under the tree bark. The latex is collected and processed into solid rubber for making tyres and other products including hosepipes and surgical gloves. Indonesia, Malaysia and Thailand together produce 72 per cent of the world's natural rubber.

Monocultures have low biodiversity. Agricultural chemicals to clear weeds and pests from crops harm wildlife, remove their habitat, and pollute water. One example of sustainable monoculture farming in South-East Asia is keeping fish in paddies to eat rice pests without using chemicals. Farmers can eat or sell the fish, too.

Key

	Oil field
	Coalfield
	Gas field
	Deciduous woodland
	Tropical rainforest
	Mountains
	Rice
0	Rubber
	Wheat
	Maize
	Fruit
	Cotton
	Cocoa
	Sugar
	Tea

NORTH KOREA

JAPAN
•Tokyo

ngyang
Seoul

SOUTH KOREA

anghai

Pacific Ocean

ipei

WAN

•Manila

PHILIPPINES

PAPUA NEW GUINEA
New Guinea
•Port Moresby

Celebes

•Dili
EAST TIMOR
Bali

Cups attached to these rubber trees in a Malaysian plantation collect the latex sap oozing from cut spiral cuts in the bark.

EXPLORE!

Around half of all rubber used does not come from trees but instead is man-made. What natural resources are synthetic rubber made from and where are they produced?

Extra rice fields have been made in Bali, Indonesia, by making terraces on steep hillsides.

0	500 miles
0	500 km

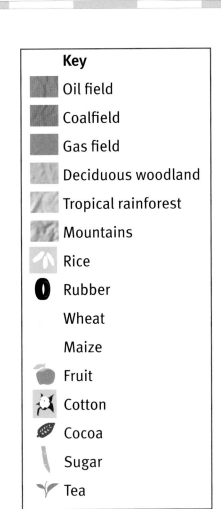
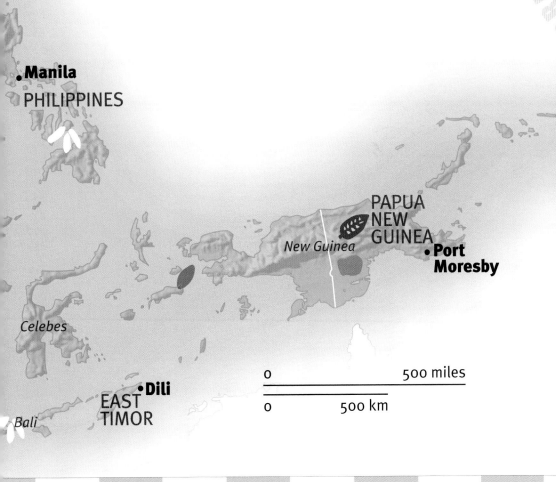

Brazil: Forest and farmland

Brazil is the leading world producer not only of oranges and coffee, grown in the south-east, but also beef and soya beans, farmed in the centre of the country. However, around 60 per cent of Brazil is covered with thick rainforest.

The Brazilian meat industry has grown rapidly over the last 20 years because it exports cheap beef around the world. Today it has over 200 million livestock. Export demand for soya beans, mostly as livestock feed but also for human consumption, is also rising in some areas.

As Brazil increases its export, farmland is created by deforestation. Mostly, the deforested areas are used for cattle ranching. Between 1996 and 2006 an area of pasture the size of Portugal was created by deforestation. Most Brazilian soya is farmed in cleared grassland, but farmers forced off this land then clear new farmland in the rainforest.

Brazil supplies 39 per cent of the total world soya bean exports, largely to China and Europe. As world population grows, so will export demand for meat and soya, driving further deforestation.

EXPLORE!
Use the Internet to find out how much soya is exported via the ports of Paranaguá and Santos. Where is it exported to?

⬆ A herd of Brazilian cattle, called Zebu, graze on newly deforested ground in the Amazon Basin. The edge of the rainforest is visible in the background.

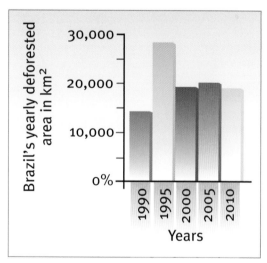

⬆ In some years, the rate of deforestation in Brazil is over three times greater than the world as a whole.

Boa Vista

Amazon Basin

Rio Trombetas

Rio Jari

Rio Paru

•Macapá

Amazon

•Belém

•Manaus

Santarém

•São Luís

•Fortaleza

Rio Madeira

Rio Sucunduri

Rio Tapajós

Rio Iriri

Rio Tocantins

•Teresina

Rio Xingu

Teles Pires

Rio Parnaíba

Natal

•riquemes

BRAZIL

Serra dos Gradas

Juazeiro do Norte •
Campina Grande •

João
Pessoa

ecis

Rio São Francisco

Recife
Maceió

•Paluas do
Tocantins

Salvador

•Cuiabá

Rio Jequitinhonha

Brasília

•Rondonópolis

•Goiânia

Brazilian Highlands

Rio Grande

Campo •
Grande

Rio Paraná

•Belo Horizonte
•Vitória

Rio Paranapanema

Campinas

Rio Ivaí

São Paulo

Rio de Janeiro

Santos

Curitiba

•Paranaguá

Rio Iguaçu

•Florianopólis

•Passo Fundo

Santa Maria

•Porto Alegre

•Rio Grande

Key	
	Tropical rainforest
	Deforestation
	Sugar cane
	Coastal woodland
	Oil field
	Coalfield
	Soya beans
	Rubber
	Maize
	Coffee
	Cocoa
	Fruit
	Cotton
	Beef cattle

0 ——— 500 miles

0 ——— 1000 km

N

North America:
Extensive farming

In North America most arable or crop farming happens in the Great Plains. This region is the world's largest producer of wheat.

The Plains were first used for arable farming because they have warm summers and adequate rainfall, and soil that retains moisture. They are also flat enough to use big machines to farm large areas extensively. Today arable farming in North America is big business. It is becoming more intensive – it requires more chemical fertilizers and pesticides to grow sufficient crops in the plains than in the past. This is due to huge amounts of crop depleting the minerals in the soil.

The growing world population needs more food and North America has little spare crop land to grow more. It is increasing productivity by using GM crops. These are crops such as maize or soya beans grown from special seeds with certain changed or modified genes. This makes the crops, for example, produce more food per plant or resist crop pests. North America produces nearly 70 per cent of the world's combined GM crop weight.

Alaska (USA)

Anchorage •

San Francisc

⬆ Wheat being harvested in Washington State, USA. The wheat fields in the USA cover about 24.2 million hectares of land.

EXPLORE!

Using GM crops is a controversial issue. What are the advantages and disadvantages of growing GM crops?

Key

Coniferous forest

Mixed farming

Arable farming, the Great Plains

Pastoral farming

Hot desert

Ice desert

Vegetable growing on irrigated farmland

See p. 21 for crop and animal symbols key

Arctic Ocean

Great Bear Lake

Northwest Territories

Great Slave Lake

Nunavut

Hudson Bay

CANADA

Alberta

Saskatchewan

Manitoba

Lake Athabasca

Lake Winnipeg

Lake Manitoba

Ontario

Québec

Labrador

Newfoundland and Labrador

Newfoundland

St Lawrence

New Brunswick

Nova Scotia

Grand Banks

British Columbia

• Edmonton

Vancouver

• Saskatoon

• Winnipeg

Seattle

ashington

North Dakota

Minnesota

Lake Superior

The Great Lakes

Lake Michigan

Lake Huron

Montréal

Maine

Cod

Herring

Hake

Montana

Wisconsin

Ottawa •

New York

• Toronto

Lake Erie

Pennsylvania

3 • Boston

5 4

• New York

New Jersey

regon

Idaho

South Dakota

Wyoming

USA

Iowa

Chicago •

Indiana

Ohio

Washington D.C.

Maryland

Delaware

Rocky Mountains

acramento

Nevada

• Denver

Nebraska

St. Louis •

Illinois

West Virginia

Virginia

East States Key
1 New Hampshire
2 Vermont
3 Massachusetts
4 Rhode Island
5 Connecticut

Utah

• Las Vegas

Colorado

Kansas

Missouri

Kentucky

North Carolina

California

Arizona

• Phoenix

New Mexico

Oklahoma

Arkansas

Tennessee

South Carolina

North Atlantic Ocean

os

ngeles

Texas

Mississippi

Alabama

Georgia

• Austin

New Orleans •

Louisiana

Florida

• Miami

Gulf of Mexico

0		500 miles

0		1000 km

27

Australia: Irrigation farming

Australia is one of the world's driest countries. Two thirds of its area is classed as arid, with insufficient rainfall for plants to grow, and much of this is barren desert. The hot, arid interior of Australia is only suitable for rearing sheep and cattle where farmers can irrigate the land.

Crops including wheat, barley, sorghum and cotton mostly grow in wetter New South Wales and Victoria, but big, regular harvests can only be guaranteed in most areas using irrigation from both rivers and groundwater. Digging ever deeper for sufficient groundwater is causing widespread salination in Australia. This is when underground salts come to the surface making soil useless for crops or pasture.

When soil damaged by salination, livestock trampling, and pesticide pollution dries up, it can crumble and blow away, so farmland turns to desert. Desertification threatens 70 per cent of Australia's farmland. Sustainable farming and water conservation are vital if agriculture for Australians and for export is to survive into the future.

Ashburton River

Perth•

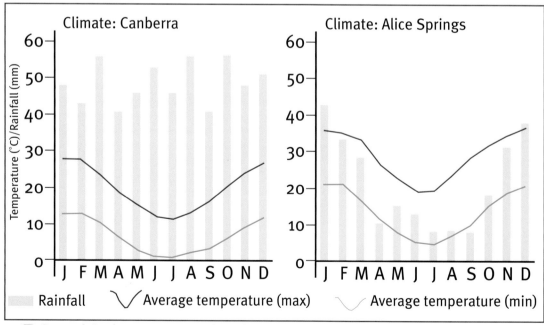

⬆ Coastal Canberra, New South Wales, has rain through the year caused by moist air blown from the ocean, but Alice Springs has a typical arid to desert climate.

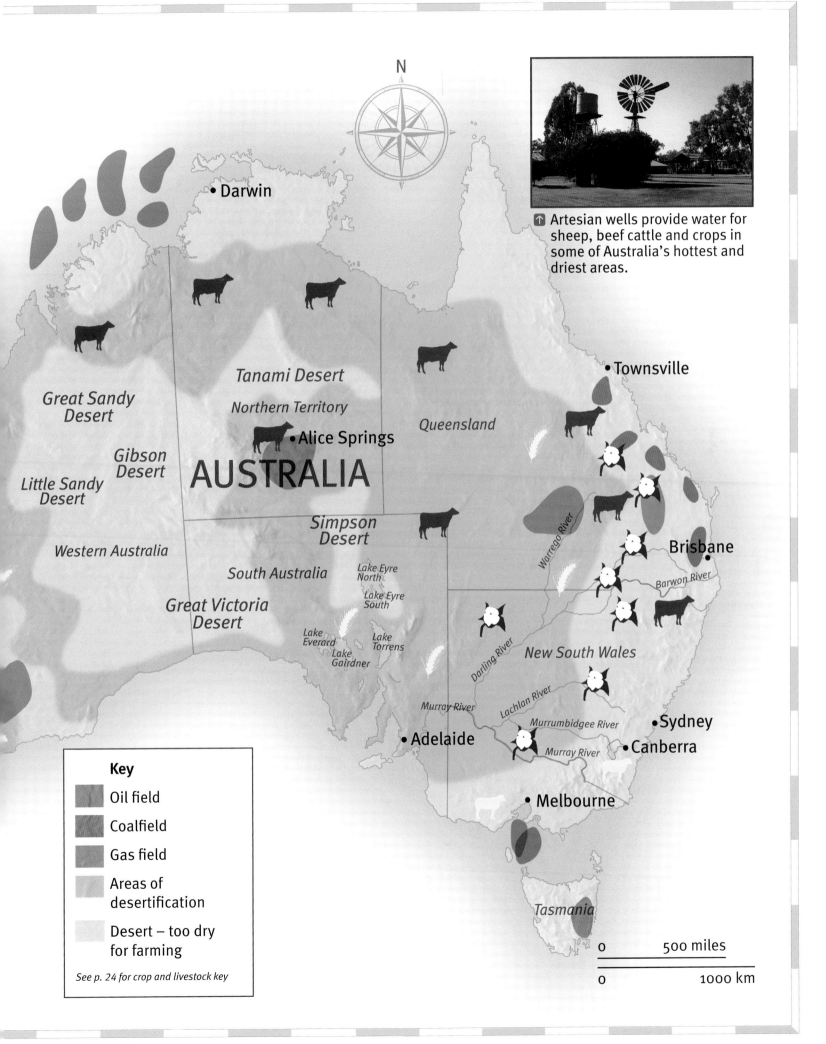

N

• Darwin

Artesian wells provide water for sheep, beef cattle and crops in some of Australia's hottest and driest areas.

Great Sandy Desert

Tanami Desert

Northern Territory

Gibson Desert

Little Sandy Desert

AUSTRALIA

• Alice Springs

Queensland

• Townsville

Western Australia

Simpson Desert

South Australia

Lake Eyre North

Lake Eyre South

Warrego River

Brisbane

Barwon River

Great Victoria Desert

Lake Everard

Lake Gairdner

Lake Torrens

Darling River

New South Wales

Lachlan River

Murray River

Murrumbidgee River

• Adelaide

Murray River

• Sydney

• Canberra

• Melbourne

Key

Oil field

Coalfield

Gas field

Areas of desertification

Desert – too dry for farming

See p. 24 for crop and livestock key

Tasmania

0   500 miles

0   1000 km

Now test yourself!

These questions will help you to revisit some of the information in this book. To answer the questions, you will need to use the contents on page 2 and the index on page 32, as well as the relevant pages on each topic.

1 Use the contents on page 2 to find which pages show a map of:

(a) Europe's main fishing areas.

(b) the largest farming areas in the USA.

(c) the most southerly place on the Earth's surface.

2 Use the index on page 32 to find the pages which will tell you:

(a) which parts of the world don't have enough water for people to live in.

(b) how paper is made from wood.

(c) how people in Bali can grow rice on steep hillsides.

3 Use the glossary on page 31 to complete a copy of this table:

Key word	Meaning of this word
	The loss of forest due to chopping down large numbers of trees.
Ecosystem	
	Rocks that have useful metals in them.
	Woodlands which grow in cool places like the British Isles.

4 Use page 4 to find out how long people can survive without any food or water.

5 Use page 8 to find out what ores contain.

6 Use page 14 to list any three industrial raw materials and what they are used to make.

7 Use page 28 to find out which farm animal is produced in very large numbers by Australia.

8 Antarctica is a continent, but the Arctic is not. Use pages 16 and 17 to find out why.

9 Which country produces most of the world's:

(a) diamonds?

(b) rice?

(c) tropical hardwoods, such as mahogany?

10 How is the world's increasing population putting pressure on its natural resources?

Glossary

chronic lasting for a long time

climate change any long-term significant changes to the weather pattern of a certain area. Climate change can have natural causes, such as volcano eruptions, and is also the result of global warming.

coniferous an evergreen tree with cones

deciduous a deciduous tree is one that loses its leaves in the autumn

deforestation the loss of forest due to the clearing of large numbers of trees

desertification the word used to describe the spread of the world's deserts

fertile land area with soil that has all the nutrients plants need to grow healthily

finite resources resources which will run out at some time in the future

fossil fuels sources of energy (like coal, oil and gas) formed from plants and animals which died millions of years ago

global warming rising temperatures worldwide, caused by the increase of gases in the air that trap the Sun's heat near the earth.

industrial raw materials natural resources that are used to make goods

irrigation putting extra water onto the soil because there isn't enough rain to grow crops

natural resources materials such as rocks, soil and water which can be used to meet people's needs

ores rocks that have useful metals in them

recycling when waste materials are used again to make new products

sustainability using natural resources in ways which allow people to use them for much longer and cause the least damage to the natural environment

tropical rainforests dense forests which grow in hotter, wetter places nearer to the Equator

water deficit when people don't have all the water they need

water surplus when people have more water than they need

Index

First published in 2011 by Wayland
Copyright © Wayland 2011

Wayland
Hachette Children's Books
338 Euston Road
London NW1 3BH

Wayland Australia
Level 17/207
Kent Street
Sydney, NSW 2000

All rights reserved.

Editor: Julia Adams
Designer: Rob Walster, Big Blu Design
Cover design: Wayland
Map Art: Martin Sanders
Illustrations: Andy Stagg
Picture research: Kathy Lockley/ Julia Adams

The website addresses (URLs) included in this book were valid at the time of going to press. However, it is possible that contents or addresses may have changed since the publication of this book No responsibility for any such changes can be accepted by either the author or the Publisher.

British Library Cataloguing in Publication Data
Gillett, Jack.
    Maps of the environmental world.
    Natural resources.
    1. Natural resources--Juvenile literature. 2. Natural resources--Maps for children.
    I. Title II. Gillett, Meg.
    333.7-dc22

ISBN 978 0 7502 6238 5

Printed in Malaysia

Wayland is a division of Hachette Children's Books, an Hachette UK company.
www.hachette.co.uk

Picture acknowledgements:
All photography: Shutterstock, except: p. 10: Jack and Meg Gillett; p. 13, p. 24: iStock Images; p. 17: Paul Andrew Lawrence / Alamy

Maps of the Environmental World

Contents of titles in the series:

WAYLAND